Profile of a Successful Entrepreneur

Profile of a Successful Entrepreneur

by
Bud (Coach Bud) Coggins

Bud (Coach Bud) Coggins

All Rights Reserved. No part of this publication may be reproduced in any form or by any means, including scanning, photocopying, or otherwise without prior written permission of the copyright holder except in the case of brief quotations embodied in critical articles and reviews.

Copyright Bud Coggins © 2018

ISBN: 978-1-944662-33-2

Cover Design by Jer Warren © 2018

Dedication

I am forever grateful to my parents, Myrtle and Wyatt Coggins, for instilling in me honesty, integrity, and service to others by their actions. My wife, Nancy, has always been supportive of me and my many ventures—successful and not so successful. This book is made possible by the many people that I have had the pleasure to coach and share their experiences.

Entrepreneurs and Eagles

Independent

Free

Courageous

Resilient

Resourceful

Risk accepting

These are the characteristics of two species: the human species we call "entrepreneur" and the bird species we know as the North American Bald Eagle. What better icon for an entrepreneur could there possibly be? For centuries this majestic bird has been a symbol of power, courage, freedom and independence. Unlike most species of birds, the eagle is a loner. While the eagle can and must rely totally on its own devices to survive, as an entrepreneur in today's crowded, competitive marketplace, it is tough to go it alone.

Fortunately, we don't have to do that unless by choice. With the advent of the high-technology era, opportunities abound to form compatible win-win alliances, partnerships, joint ventures and other creative ways to help each other succeed. As entrepreneurs, when we "flock" together, we raise our level of success.

One of our greatest strengths is also one of our greatest weaknesses. With our passion for independence, our resourcefulness, resilience and a dash of ego, we think we can do it all without help.

Bud (Coach Bud) Coggins

This attitude becomes even more prevalent when we realize others around us don't have the same passionate feeling for what we are doing and embrace our vision. The sooner we understand that we can realize our dreams by giving and receiving help, the faster our journey of success becomes. My mantra is and always will be, "When your true purpose is to help others succeed …you succeed."

Acknowledgments

I am grateful to the talented and professional people who contributed to creating this book. My good friend and coach Drew Becker of Realization Press is my guiding light, who provided his book publishing expertise. I also wish to thank Lillian D. Henderson, editor, Jer Warren, graphic designer, and Website Designer Chris Basnight of IMP Designs. All quotes came from Dr. Nido R. Qubein's book, *Change Your Words, Change Your World* which you can order at *nidoqubein.com*. Dr. Qubein is president of High Point University and a world renowned speaker.

About Coach Bud

At the age of 48, with a son in college and two daughters in high school, Bud Coggins (aka Coach Bud) left the security of the corporate world (yes, in 1984 when there was job security) to pursue his passion for independence, part of his family DNA.

After a 21-year career in television broadcasting, he started Coggins Sales and Marketing, Inc. to help small business owners achieve their pursuit of a successful venture.

His experiences of the last 40+ years coaching entrepreneurs have earned him an LBD (Learn by Doing) degree in the entrepreneurial world.

His stated purpose is "Helping Entrepreneurs Achieve Success." This purpose is manifest by sharing his experiences with those who seek real-world information to enhance their journey of success.

In 2011, the company name was changed to Coggins Communications, LLC, to better reflect the company focus. In 2017, the company was renamed CoachBudsEntrepreneursU.

His information is shared through individual coaching, workshops, articles, books, e-books, radio and television, and Coach Bud's Blog.

Coming soon is CoachBudsEntrepreneursU membership website with a wealth of information to help small business owners and aspiring entrepreneurs enhance their success. Stay tuned.

CoachBudsEntrepreneursU

Helping Entrepreneurs Achieve Success

www.coachbudsbooks.com

cb@entrepreneursu.com

About This Book

"Look before you leap." This very old adage is extremely applicable to your intention to enter or stay in the "Real World of the Entrepreneur." You have much looking to do *before* you leap.

The content of the book is focused on "Why become an entrepreneur?" There are many resources available to address the "how." However, in our high tech world, this is irrelevant until you are able to answer the "why" honestly and objectively.

In my 40+ years of being and coaching entrepreneurs, I have confirmed that the number one reason that fifty (50%) of "startup" small businesses fail in their first year is a lack of understanding of what it takes mentally, emotionally, physically, and financially to survive and thrive.

Your journey *must* begin with thorough and objective due diligence to determine if your idea for a product or service is valid. Your brother-in-law telling you that it is the "best idea since sliced bread" does not qualify as due diligence. In the highly technical world we live in today, information on any subject you can think of is available; do your research.

Ask trusted sources, people who have "been there and done that," to share their experiences. Keep in mind that you will be putting your future, family, and finances at risk. If this all sounds too daunting and overwhelming, that is not my intent.

I am not here to persuade or dissuade you from realizing your dream. My purpose is to encourage you to look before you leap. I encourage you to read this entire book before taking the "Profile of a Successful Entrepreneur Self-Assessment." To have value, your responses must be honest and objective to help you decide if becoming an entrepreneur is the journey you know is meant for you.

This book is a collection of previously-published articles in magazines, newspapers, blogs and printed books. The content is original and reflects Coach Bud's real world experiences as an entrepreneur.

There are no theories in this book. It was created to provide you with practical, timeless, strategic, and tactical information to help you on your journey of success. It's up to your discretion to decide what is helpful to you.

My hope is that you will glean valuable information to help you survive and thrive.

This is the first in a series of Coach Bud's "Helping Entrepreneurs Achieve Success" books addressing various business and inspirational topics.

Table of Contents

CHAPTER ONE Inspirational 1

If Only 2

Creating an Impact with Your Life and Legacy 4

America—Our Entrepreneurial Spirit 10

The Procrastinator's Mantra: I'm going to... 13

Listen to Your Heart by Bud Coggins 18

CHAPTER TWO Developing Your Game Plan, A to Z 23

Business Partnerships 29

CHAPTER THREE Communication 33

3 Cs + 3 Ms = Effective Communication 33

CHAPTER FOUR Marketing 41

What Is Marketing? 42

The Power of Effective Networking 45

Go with the Pros 50

The 4 Ps of Successful Showcasing 55

CHAPTER FIVE Advertising 61

What Is Advertising? 61

Advertising Options 62

Bud (Coach Bud) Coggins

CHAPTER SIX S\ALES 65

Universal Sales Purpose...66

Selling is a Slam Dunk—with the Right Attitude!.........................72

Fill the Pipeline...24/7/365 77

CHAPTER SEVEN C\USTOMER S\ERVICE 81

The Customer Is Boss or You Are Fired. 81

ASSESSMENT 87

Entrepreneur Compatibility Self-Assessment 87

Special Offer..91

CHAPTER ONE
Inspirational

"If Only"

Creating an Impact with Your Life and Legacy

America—Our Entrepreneurial Spirit

The Procrastinator's Mantra

Listen to Your Heart

Bud (Coach Bud) Coggins

If Only

If only I had known
That you would soon be gone,
That this was your last time out the door,
I would have prayed for so much more.
I would have held you in my arms
And asked that God keep you from harm.
If only I had known
This was your final dawn,
If I'd had some kind of sign,
I would have cried out to the Divine,
"Lord, give us just a bit more time."
If only I had known,
I'd tell you how much I had grown
From knowing you, my friend,
And if it were up to me our time would never end.
If only I had known
That God would call you Home,
That from this world you must depart,
I would have given all my heart,
Every ounce of love I could impart.
But tomorrow lies unknown—
Its seeds have yet to be sewn,

And we cannot know that final date;
We mortals simply have to wait.
So let us live each and every day
Sharing kindness in every way.
Let us make this conscious vow
To live in gratitude here and now,
Showing our dear ones that we care
And spreading love everywhere.

NOTE:

This powerful, thoughtful, and provoking poem was written by my editor, Lillian D. "Diana" Henderson. It brings to mind the great loss of life on 9/11. For all of us who lived that horror, our lives were changed forever. This poem reminds us to live fully today and always express what is in our hearts to those we cherish.

Creating an Impact with Your Life and Legacy

Have you ever asked yourself, "What is my true purpose in life? What will my legacy be?"

People the world over have wrestled with these questions since time began. For some people these are answered at a young age; for others, later in life. For the majority they are never answered.

On life's journey we are presented with opportunities to answer these questions, but either we don't see them or we choose to ignore the signs.

I, for one, believe that everything happens for a reason. Many times, we wonder why something (good or bad) is happening to us and realize years later the reason.

I recognize that my over 40 years of experiences in "The Real World of an Entrepreneur" were meant to be shared with readers to help make the path to success smoother by knowing the challenges you will face.

This book is a prime example of a *meant to be* project. Over many years of real world experiences, my own and those gained from coaching other entrepreneurs; articles I've written; books; radio and TV programs; blogs and seminars I've presented, I realized part of my purpose is to share all this information with others to help them succeed.

Reflecting on those many years of experience, personal and business, I offer a formula that I believe can serve as a guideline to life's journey.

Integrity

Someone once said, "Integrity is doing the right thing when nobody will ever know."

I am forever indebted to my parents for instilling integrity in me, not by telling but by living as an example. I believe that integrity is the foundation of our core values. In a world full of challenges, it's our integrity that helps us meet and overcome any obstacle to inner peace.

Mentoring

Webster's Dictionary defines a mentor as a "wise and trusted counselor." We can all be a mentor at any age. There is always someone who needs to know what we know. It is my opinion that we all have an obligation to share our knowledge, gained mostly through experiences, with others who have not yet "been there and done that." Everyone is proficient at something and needs to share their expertise with those who need to know in order to make their lives better. Often, you learn as much from your mentee as they learn from you.

Passion

The driving force for every positive outcome, your passion can only be determined by *you*. When you feel beaten down and ready to give up, your passion inspires you to keep going. Don't let negative people or circumstances impact your passion.

Passion kept Thomas Edison on track to invent the light bulb. When asked by a newspaper reporter, "Mr. Edison, how can you keep going when you have failed 5,000 times," Edison responded, "That, sir, is incorrect. I now know there are 5,000 ways it won't work."

There are many obstacles on an entrepreneur's journey to building a successful business. With a clear purpose and an uncompromising passion for that purpose driving you, failure is not an option.

A caution about "blind passion" based on my own experience: You can have such a strong desire for an idea that you are blinded and unable to see the facts. A thorough due diligence of the viability of the idea is necessary if you are to make an informed decision whether to go forward or not.

Ask yourself, "Is there a market for my idea, and do I have the resources for funding, experiences, expertise, contacts, etc. to create a successful venture?"

The formula for a successful venture is: a clear purpose, an uncompromising passion for your purpose and a thorough due diligence process to examine the facts and make an informed decision.

Attitude

This is deal maker or breaker in any situation. Whether you have a positive or negative attitude is totally your choice. People and circumstances can affect your choice, but ultimately *you* are the creator of your attitude. We all know that a positive attitude will result in the best outcome for any situation.

So, why are so many people consumed by a negative attitude? Could it be ego? Could it be their environment? Could it be their level of education? Could it be a victim mentality? Could it be "win at all cost" thinking? I'm not a judge or jury; I just know that each of us has the option to choose our attitude. I choose positive. How about you?

Communication

Communication is the major factor determining the outcome of any situation. Simply put, the more effective a communicator you are, the more success you enjoy.

The good news is that effective communication is a learned skill. The most important aspect is learning to be a good listener. A good listener is the person who focuses on the complete message. He or she doesn't interrupt and processes the message before responding. For those of us who are highly verbal, this requires discipline.

Poor communication skills are the root cause of most problems and negative outcomes, including dissolutions of relationships (personal and business).

Trust

The foundation of any relationship, personal or business, is trust. People the world over want to be friends with and do business with someone they can trust. Trust must be earned by demonstration, not by words alone. In business, trust, not price, is the deal maker. If you are viewed by your customers as a "commodity" that they can get from others, their buying decisions are most likely to be based on price. You can't build a small business by being the "lowest price guy." Leave that to the Walmarts of the world.

Trust is the main reason people do business with you. Think about the people with whom you do business.

In conclusion, I believe implementing the characteristics and skills outlined in this writing will create a life and legacy in which you will find peace within and success.

There is a great book entitled, *The Dash*, by Linda Ellis and Mac Anderson (*www.walkthetalk.com*) that puts your life and legacy in perspective. The dash is the space between the date of your birth and the date of your death.

The Dash is best described by Mac Anderson. "We do not choose to be born. We do not choose our parents or the country of our birth. We do not, most of us, choose to die, nor do we choose the time and conditions of our death. However, within this realm of choicelessness, we do choose *how* we live."

How will you live your dash? As you read this book, keep the above core values in mind as a guide to your thinking and action.

A legacy is what you bequeath to humanity. If it's a good legacy, its benefits will remain long after your name has been forgotten.

- Nido R Qubein

Bud (Coach Bud) Coggins

America — Our Entrepreneurial Spirit

As a lad of five years, the first life-changing event I faced occurred on December 7, 1941, when President Franklin Delano Roosevelt announced to the nation on radio (no TV then) that the Japanese Empire had staged an unprovoked air attack on our naval base at Pearl Harbor in the Hawaiian Islands. Many American military lives were lost and our entry into WWII was declared.

Growing up in wartime, I learned very early in life what the "American Spirit" was all about. At my young age, it was difficult to understand why our young men and women had to die in a distant land. I eventually came to comprehend that they were sacrificing their lives so that I could grow up safe and be secure in a country that values freedom, independence and the opportunity to make choices.

History will record, as it has throughout my life, that as tragic and despicable as the events of September 11, 2001, were, the determination, will and resolve of the American people will prevail.

We will always remember the heroes who inspired us to move on with a renewed sense of importance in our personal and professional lives. The accounts of unselfish heroism will require a separate book from the collection of history books. The same traits that characterize our American spirit also define our entrepreneurial spirit.

While the magnitude pales in comparison to terrorism, we entrepreneurs face daily challenges that test our will and resolve; yet, we overcome, learn and grow as we continue our journey of success.

The entrepreneurial spirit of our country continues to make us the greatest nation on earth and provides us the freedom to pursue our passion for independence and make a difference in the lives of others.

According to *Webster's Dictionary*, an entrepreneur is "a person who organizes and manages any enterprise, especially a business, usually with considerable initiative and risk."

Christopher Columbus set the foundation for entrepreneurism by pursuing, at great risk, his vision of a different world. Much later, the Pilgrims risked their lives to create a society free to worship and free of oppression.

Often we forget the so-called "giants" of industry also began their businesses as entrepreneurial ventures fueled by a vision to create a better world. Our history books portray the likes of Thomas Edison, Henry Ford, Andrew Carnegie, the Vanderbilts, and many others.

With the combination of a cooling economy and the world-changing events of September 11, this was an important time to pause, reflect and review the current status of your business.

Since many uncertainties still lie ahead, we must adjust our thinking and plan various scenarios to cope with and survive this new world we now live in.

One attitude adjustment many companies need to make is how they view their customers (internally and externally). When you demonstrate to your customers that you value their business in good times, they are more likely to stay with you in bad times. Everyone wins in a customer-focused environment.

Depending upon the markets served, some organizations will have to slightly alter the way business is conducted, and others may need to make radical changes. Either way, every ounce of creativity and innovative thinking we can muster is required. Huge egos and attitudes of self- interest cannot continue.

Leadership is paramount to success. As has been the case many times in the past, I am uncertain about the immediate future, but I have no doubts that the entrepreneurial spirit that exists in America will prevail.

Entrepreneurs have many new challenges to face; yet, if we open our hearts, eyes, ears, minds, renew our passion and determination that got us here, and make the necessary adjustments to attain the success we strive for, just like America, we will continue to live, work and thrive in "the land of the free and home of the brave."

Profile of a Successful Entrepreneur

The Procrastinator's Mantra: I'm going to...

"I'm going to quit smoking at midnight on Sunday."

"I'm going to go on a diet soon."

Do these declarations sound familiar to you? "I'm going to_____ (fill in the blank).

Let those who have not uttered these words over and over be the first to cast aspersions on those of us who are card-carrying procrastinators.

The question is why do we have to be hit upside the head with a 2 x 4 before we actually take action and right a behavior we know is wrong for us? How can seemingly intelligent people continue to do stupid things that are harmful to their health?

I'm not here to provide a clinical answer, but to ponder the reasons we knowingly continue damaging behavior.

Since Sir Walter Raleigh "discovered" North Carolina, it has been a birthright to smoke tobacco products. After all, they did name a cigarette after him.

Even in the early 1960s, it was a secret that smoking could possibly be harmful to your health. As evidence began to come out of the closet, the U.S. Congress banned cigarette advertising from television broadcasting and required Public Service Announcements encouraging people to stop smoking.

The culture of North Carolina began to change. In 1968, I was smoking four, yes four, packs of cigarettes per day. People would say,

"How can you possibly smoke eighty cigarettes a day?" My response was, "I have to get up early and stay up late."

At midnight August 18, 1968, 1 pulled my last nasty drag of the "weed." For me, going cold turkey was the only way. Five of my associates and I signed an agreement that whoever started back smoking would pay the others $25 each. Remember, this was 1968 when $25 got you a lot more than a couple gallons of gas and a small latte at your favorite coffee shop.

Only one other associate and I celebrated our 50th anniversary of not smoking in 2018. I am 100% convinced that I would not be here to tell this story today if I had not quit smoking. The irony is that as a totally positive person I survived withdrawal by focusing on the negative aspects of smoking. Burned holes in clothing, stale smoke in car and office, and yellow fingers were compelling reasons not to smoke.

But the real clincher was the constant plea of my two small children, who were asking, "Daddy, why do you smoke?" Try answering that question to a four and a two-year-old.

An offshoot to not smoking was a constant struggle to maintain weight control. All of a sudden, food really tasted good. So, a war against weight began a long, hard fought battle. Three children (one born in '69) grew up hearing me declare, "I'm going to start my diet on Monday." I could not begin to count the number of Mondays that "started my diet."

One of the great mysteries of life is that we know intellectually that a "diet" never works for most people. Emotionally, we are sure we can lose a quick fifteen pounds and then return to those wonderful treats we sacrificed while dieting.

Wake up and smell the hummus. It doesn't work that way. We each have to discover what inspires us to make changes that we know need to be made.

On August 30, 2002, I was really jolted by a heart attack that came with no warning. Over the years since 1968, I have constantly maintained at least a moderate exercise regimen an average of three days a week. Additionally, I have eaten fairly healthy food.

Fortunately, my cardiac event was a big warning. I got another chance that many people don't get when having a heart attack. My cardiologist determined that with medication, increased exercise, and a new approach to nutrition, I should live.

In the ensuing six months, I was involved in a cardiac rehab exercise program at an outstanding medical facility that specializes in heart disease, made permanent healthy lifestyle changes in my nutrition (by the way, hummus doesn't taste like "earth" as I once thought) and lost twenty pounds.

My inspiration was once again thinking of the negative outcome (like a shortened life) of not making lifestyle changes.

More importantly, a loving, caring wife and nine beautiful grandchildren are inspiration enough to hang around for as many years as I have control over. The good news is that healthy foods don't taste like the carton they came in as they once did.

Even though we are still a nation of extreme obesity, food manufacturers have found a market in those of us who have been whacked upside the head with the proverbial 2 x 4.

Ask yourself, "What inspiration do I need to rekindle my heart, soul, and body?" Once you make this discovery and take action, your self-worth will skyrocket.

As Benjamin Disraeli stated over 150 years ago, "The secret of success is consistency of purpose." Have you discovered your life's purpose?

Update: On August 18, 2018, one of my colleagues and I celebrated 50 years of not smoking. As an extra incentive, I now have nine grandchildren ranging from age 11 to 24. While I still carry my "Professional Procrastinator's Card," I don't play it on issues that really matter.

As the old adage says, "Where there is a will, there is a way."

Profile of a Successful Entrepreneur

Procrastination is delaying anything you need or want to do until later—when there is no valid reason to do so.

-Nido R. Qubein

Bud (Coach Bud) Coggins

Listen to Your Heart
by Bud Coggins

WakeMed heart patient Bud Coggins shares his story about his battle with heart disease and successful recovery.

My story begins on a warm, muggy August 2002 morning. I was having routine maintenance performed on my car. I began to feel nauseous but no pain. I drove home and when I walked in the door, Nancy (my wife) said, "You're pale as a ghost; what's wrong?" By then I was sweating but still had no pain.

Being a nurse, she recognized the symptoms of a heart attack and gave me an aspirin. I had no previous problems or warning of a heart attack. So, off to WakeMed we went straight to the Emergency Room.

Dr. Amarendra Reddy of WakeMed Faculty Physicians-Raleigh Cardiology was on ER duty and immediately scheduled a heart catheterization.

The cath indicated 40 percent blockage in two arteries. Another artery was 100 percent blocked and had already formed its own bypass.

The good news was that no invasive procedures were necessary. I went on medications such as Plavix® (blood thinner) to help keep my arteries open to blood flow.

After the *event*, I stepped up my exercise and began paying very close attention to my eating habits. Subsequently, every year I have had a heart check and all appeared good.

Then, along came late November 2012. Nancy and I were doing our usual workout. We were on treadmills, side by side, when I had an unusual shortness of breath. I thought that I had increased the treadmill speed beyond my usual speed.

With Nancy's strong urging, I decided to call for an appointment with Dr. Reddy the next day to check it out. The appointments secretary said Dr. Reddy was booked until December 19. I said, "I think I better come before that." So, she double-checked and found a cancellation for two days later that had just opened up.

I went to the appointment thinking I might need a stent. After an EKG and further examination, Dr. Reddy determined that a catheterization would confirm what was going on with my heart. The cath was set for the next day.

Well, the cath revealed that I had 99 percent blockage in two main arteries and 70 percent in another, commonly referred to as a "widow maker." In other words, I was a walking time bomb. I would not have left the hospital that day and surgery would have been scheduled ASAP.

However, because I was on Plavix (blood thinner) we had to delay the surgery for seven days until the Plavix was out of my bloodstream. The risk of complications was too high if we proceeded with the surgery.

The cardiac surgeon, Dr. William Killinger, described my situation as an avalanche on a snowy mountain. You don't know when it is going to come down, but it is going to come down eventually. He suggested we get a prescription of nitrate pills, go home and just wait for seven days.

Fortunately, no *event* occurred and we went to WakeMed early on the morning of December 11, 2012, for the surgery. As we pulled into the parking area and got to the entrance door, Nancy breathed a sigh of relief and exclaimed, "Okay, now you are theirs."

Dr. Killinger performed a triple bypass and all went well. The next seven days were pretty rough, but Nancy was by my side 24-7 and I kept my focus on the fact that without the surgery the odds were that I would not live long.

Nancy and I believe—and have many occurrences to support that belief—that everything happens for a reason. We may not know or understand the reason, but I got a second chance at life and am grateful for it.

A couple days before I was to leave the hospital, Dr. Reddy saw that my heartbeat was irregular and I needed a procedure to shock my heart back into rhythm. The procedure, which had some risk involved, was scheduled for the next day.

As we prepared for it, my room was filled with a large team of professionals including the "crash cart." I had just signed the consent form for the anesthesiologist and was a minute away from being put under sedation.

At that moment, Dr. Reddy rushed into the room and said, "Stop everything; his heart is back in rhythm and all is well."

Since it was the Christmas season, we labeled the occurrence, "The Christmas Miracle on New Bern Avenue."

The old adage that "all is well that ends well" certainly applied to this situation.

As a side note, I had none of the usual pain at all and required no pain medicine after the surgery.

We came home on December 19. You will recall that was initially the earliest appointment to see Dr. Reddy. Divine intervention? Go figure.

I completed my 12-week Cardiac Rehab program at WakeMed, being assisted by an awesome team of health professionals. Nancy and I continue to exercise three times a week.

I shall be ever grateful to Dr. Reddy and Dr. Killinger for saving my life. The message of my story is that your heart may not scream for help. Even if it whimpers, go immediately to your cardiologist. Bottom line: "Listen to your Heart."

Accept each moment as a gift to be received with joy.

-Nido R. Qubein

CHAPTER TWO
Developing Your Game Plan, A to Z

In any sport there is always a Coach who uses their experiences to formulate a Game Plan on a practical, non-emotional basis.

Incorporating my 40+ years of experiences as an Entrepreneur and Coach, I am your Coach to guide you through your Game Plan.

Your Game Plan, to be effective, MUST be based on objective, honest, non-emotional facts. This requires discipline at a time when your excitement regarding your idea is peaking. At the same time, you must have a "True Passion" for your idea. This is not easy.

However, the more you follow this plan, the more successful you will be. Focus on the "end game."

Due Diligence to determine:

Your "Journey" begins with a thorough process of Due Diligence

A. What is the true purpose of my idea? Your written Purpose Statement is your guiding principal to everything that you do. Example: Coach Bud's Written Purpose Statement is "Helping Entrepreneurs Achieve Success" Coach Bud's favorite saying is, "When your true purpose is helping others succeed...you succeed"

B. Along with your Written Purpose Statement comes an uncompromising Passion for your idea. Caution: Don't let your passion blind you from reality. Your "Passion" is essential when the tough times come (and they will).

C. Does my idea already exist? if so, will my idea be an improvement? Be sure your idea is not already patented or copyrighted. If not, patent or copyright your idea immediately. Use a Patent Attorney to file for you. Don't reveal your idea to anyone (especially your Brother-in-Law) until it is legally protected.

D. Who would purchase my idea? Why would they purchase from me? This answer lies in your targeted prospect and their needs and your solutions. As you build a positive reputation, you will find that clients will refer you to others.

E. What/Who will be my competition? Determine by your research

F. How will I fund my idea? How much do I need? This determination is necessary before you launch your idea. Explore all options. Loans are not easy to get. Your personal, positive credit score will help.

Profile of a Successful Entrepreneur

G. Can I be a 'Solo Entrepreneur" or do I need a Partner(s)? This is an extremely important question. My recommendation is that you exhaust every possible option to maintain 100% ownership of your idea. It would take another entire book to address the complexities of this subject. Maybe that's my next book. Stay tuned...

H. Will my Spouse/Family need to support my idea? The answer is absolutely YES! You must consider that when you decide to "go for it," you are risking a fixed income, security, your and their future with unknown results. My purpose for this book is not to scare you away from becoming an Entrepreneur but, to share the "Real World" experiences you will face. The number one reason I have discovered why the statistics show that a start-up business has a 50% chance of survival the first year is because they go unknowingly into what it takes to survive and thrive.

I. Do I need an Attorney? It depends on your industry and state/city and their amount of regulations you must abide by.

J. Do I need a CPA or Accountant? It depends on the volume of bookkeeper activities are necessary and your financial expertise

K. What Business Licenses do I need? You can check with your industry's Organization, Attorney or CPA

L. Is the industry of my idea regulated? Check it out.

M. Can I operate in a Home-Based office or need office location? The answer is a financial consideration or if your

Client/Customer visits your office, you must have an out-of-home office.

N. Do I need to have Marketing & Sales experience? It certainly is a BIG plus if you have experience. If not, your Community College most likely offers classes (free or low cost). Contract with a person you know and trust who has experience in Sales and or Marketing. Also, follow the process described in the book (*Be A Solutionist*).

O. Can I EARN the trust of others? You have to EARN people's trust by your actions, not just your talk. True Integrity is the key. You can't "fake it til you make it."

P. Will my Game Plan be in writing? Reviewed on a timely schedule? After your plan is solid in place, you definitely want it written. Don't just file it away. Review it quarterly to update.

Q. Will I always be guided by my core values? I hope you will.

R. Have I established my Customer Service Policy? Your policy should be in writing. Remember that the Customer/Client Service is top priority.

S. Do I have sufficient 'Social Media" skills or do I hire someone? If you are not aware of proper use of Social Media, definitely contract with someone who is proficient with how to maximize use.

T. Do I have a plan for self-development? It is extremely important for you to be up-to-date on the issues that affect your industry and/or business.

U. Based on my experiences, will I share them to help others? We all have an obligation to those who need to know what we know, Be a Mentor. Remember: "If Our True Purpose is to help others succeed... we succeed."

V. Written Plan for Mental & Physical Fitness, you can lessen the stress and concern that goes along with owning your own business by having a written plan to handle the stress.

W. Do I have the skill to create "Strategic Alliances?" This will help your business grow faster.

X. Do I have my "what ifs" planned in advance? Example a competitor comes into your Market or a competitor closes their business. What impact will that have on your business?

Y. Are my communication skills sufficient? Communication skills are learned. See The 3 C's and 3M's of Communication in this book.

Z. What is my business exit plan? Will to family? Sell to another individual or company?

My goal is not to persuade or dissuade you from being an Entrepreneur but, to share "Real World" experiences to help you determine if you are a match. If you approach this book with an open mind, objectivity, honest answers to questions, YOU will KNOW if you've made the right decision.

Successful people don't avoid risks. They learn to manage them. They don't dive off cliffs into unexplored waters; they learn how deep the water is and make sure there are no hidden obstacles. Then they plunge in.

-Nido R. Qubein

Business Partnerships

This information is based on my 40+ years experiences as an entrepreneur and coach of many other entrepreneurs. There are many options to create partnerships and we will explore them.

I label them as "Good, Bad and Ugly." Before considering a partnership, it is imperative that your thorough due diligence is complete.

Good:

If you can be a solo entrepreneur and retain 100% ownership with your own funds or a loan, nothing is better than that. Be aware that many hurdles have to be jumped to acquire a loan. You may have to hire a qualified consultant that provides a service you lack experience in (e.g., sales and marketing).

If you can, attract a silent partner, someone who will invest in your business without giving you input and will trust you to make them money.

Good or Bad

If you decide that you need a permanent partner, you should do the following:

Whether you know the potential partner or not, you should conduct due diligence with this in mind:

Each of you should conduct and share:

A. Profile of a Successful Entrepreneur Self-Assessment

B. A personality profile (DISC) to determine compatibility

C. Background check on both of you

D. Personal/business references

E. Personal financial statement

F. Meeting with spouses & family

G. Funding resources

H. Meeting with an attorney

I. Meeting with an accountant or CPA

J. Physical examination

K. Meeting with an attorney to complete written Operating Agreement

L. Roles and responsibilities

M. Compensation

N. Hiring/firing procedures

O. Insurance required

P. Shared values

Q. Decision making process

R. Buy/sell agreement

S. Written purpose of the company

T. Written game plan

U. Review of written plan process

V. Exit strategy

Ugly

Having two or more other partners can bring significant problems. Even if they bring a different expertise, there is a high chance it will lead to a two-against-one situation at some point. I know this from personal experience. When you are excited about the situation, step back and be realistic about the idea.

Anytime you need a person with experience in a particular issue, be sure you consult with someone you trust to refer you to their trusted source.

You may feel overwhelmed with this process. However, remember that you are putting your future, your money, and your family at stake. "Look before you leap."

CHAPTER THREE
Communication

3 Cs + 3 Ms = Effective Communication

When we pause and reflect on the significance of communication, we realize that effective communication impacts our business and personal success more than any other factor.

In one form or another, communication permeates all that we do and say. Whether it's internal to employees, external to customers/prospects, or in personal interaction, our ability to communicate effectively determines the results.

Words, actions, and body language have a powerful impact, good or bad, on those with whom we communicate.

If we look back in history and examine the characteristics of great world leaders, we find one common trait among all: They were effective communicators. You may not want to be among the world's great leaders, but you can greatly enhance your success by becoming an effective communicator.

All it takes is a focus on honing your abilities. With the right mindset, you can acquire the necessary skills by a commitment to working on developing them.

As a beginning, let's explore the foundational elements that will have an immediate impact on communication success.

The three Cs of Effective Communication

Whether you are communicating by the spoken or written word, keep these three essential elements in mind:

Clarity: Insure that what you are saying or writing is clear to the intended listener/reader by thinking through the message and the response you expect to evoke.

Clarity is essential to effective communication, especially in your written communication. The reader will not have the option to question your meaning or ask for clarity. If your message is unclear, it leaves the interpretation solely in the reader's mind, which may not be the message you intended to communicate. Are we *clear* on this?

Conciseness: In the fast-paced world we live in today, brevity is cherished. Quality time is a scarce commodity. Consider using fewer words to convey your message while retaining clarity. The option to email, text, and tweet opened up a whole new world of communication. Twitter is the extreme example of being concise.

I'm sure English teachers are going ballistic over the sentence structure (or lack thereof) in most email messages. The balance for effective communication lies somewhere between voluminous, unnecessary words and the choppy words and incomplete sentences of the email, text, and tweeting world.

Consistency: Once you have developed a clear and concise message that you are satisfied conveys the reasons people will want to do business with you and your company, consistency is essential.

We are constantly bombarded with a deluge of information. It takes time for any message to get through. When you have lived with your message day in and day out and are tiring of it, your target listeners/readers are probably just beginning to *get it*.

After you are satisfied with your message, it's always a good idea to have one or more trusted source(s) (not your brother-in-law) who will be honest and objective, read your message, and give you feedback and input. You will often be in shock and awe of their interpretation.

The 3 Ms of Effective Communication

These three additional key elements are essential to effective communication:

Message: Using the three Cs above, carefully craft your message incorporating the reasons a customer or prospect should consider doing business with you and your company—from their perspective.

Develop an honest and credible message that may, depending on your type of product or service, involve features, general benefits, solutions, company principles and values, innovative ideas, user testimonials, or other factors pertinent to your product or service.

The challenge is to make your message inspiring or motivational enough to evoke a response without exaggerated claims. Be sure you communicate the *true* differentiation between what you are offering and the offers of your competitors.

Never knock or mention the name of a competitor. Focus on the positive reasons the customer/prospect will be extremely satisfied with your service.

Remember most purchasers see your product or service as a commodity. In other words, from their perspective, they can get the same product or service from your competitors sometimes for less money.

For most of us offering the lowest price is not going to create a successful business. It is essential to your success that you clearly differentiate your offering from the field of price cutters. You can't win that battle.

Message Recipient: This is the person to whom you are targeting your message. You must first know who the decision maker is for your specific product or service.

Next, you decide what response you want to evoke. Are you looking for an immediate purchase? Are you seeking an in-person appointment to determine their needs and explore ways you may be able to meet their needs?

My preference is to obtain a face-to-face meeting to help determine their needs and begin to gain their trust in you. Then, knowing their responsibilities within their company, you must determine what message is going to motivate them to respond favorably to your request.

Example: If the Chief Financial Officer is the decision maker for your product or service, your offering better save or make their company money.

Messenger

The messenger is the medium you select to deliver your carefully-crafted message to the appropriate recipient.

When you have a clear profile of your best customer/prospect, selection of the targeted medium is much easier.

Every medium has a targeted reader, listener, viewer, etc. Independent research data is available that will help you match your customer's profile to that specific medium's targeted profile.

Over my fifty years in media advertising and consulting, I have seen many misdirected dollars wasted on ineffective advertising. Your precious resources of time and money need to be targeted, focused, efficient and effective.

Be sure you incorporate the three Cs and three Ms into your communication.

Remember that a well-crafted message falls on deaf ears if not targeted to your best customer/prospect.

I would be committing a felonious crime, punishable by hanging, if I failed to mention one of the most significant elements of effective communication—true listening.

We all could fill truckloads with examples of horror stories created by others and us when they or we fail to listen carefully to the other person. Our tendency is to jump in, make snap judgments, provide solutions, make incorrect assumptions, and fast forward the other's story without focusing on what they are saying and then responding appropriately.

Bud (Coach Bud) Coggins

Silence can be golden.

I hope this material has been clear, concise, and consistent enough to inspire you to work on your communication skills. There are many resources of books, tapes, and seminars available to help you become an effective communicator.

Profile of a Successful Entrepreneur

The leader who can't communicate can't create the conditions that motivate.

- Nido R Qubein

CHAPTER FOUR
Marketing

What is Marketing?

The Power of Effective Networking

Go with The Pros

The Four Ps of Successful Showcasing

What Is Marketing?

Marketing is a multitude of various activities you conduct to communicate with your target clients or customers the solutions you provide to improve their lives and/or businesses. I have always thought of marketing as the concrete that paves the way to the sale. Marketing is *not* about you; it's about them.

Some people confuse marketing with advertising. The basic difference is that many marketing activities require low to no cash outlay—only your time.

Example: networking events

I see a lot of money wasted by people who have not done their due diligence to determine exactly who their best prospects are for their product/service before they plan their marketing.

For your marketing to be effective, you must:

1. Clearly identify who is most likely to need or want your product/service.

    A. Age

    B. Gender(s)

    C. Geographic location

    D. Industry

    E. Your competition

    F. Ethnic

2. Clearly identify the decision maker in all business transactions.

3. Determine the best media options (social media, print, radio, TV, etc.) to communicate your solutions to your prospect. All media have statistics to help you decide if they reach your target prospect's profile.

4. Make sure you follow the three Cs and three Ms of communication.

Your Marketing Plan should be focused on what you must do to accomplish the financial goals you have set in your business plan.

Bottom Line: Marketing done right can be effective, fun, productive, and profitable.

I found that one of my most effective marketing techniques was:

1. To identify a target prospect

2. Mail the prospect a letter (may have met them at a networking event)

3. Request a meeting to explore the prospect's needs (one hour, no cost, no obligation).

4. Together determine if you can provide a solution to their needs. If not, ask that person to refer you to someone they know who may need your solutions.

What you say does not have nearly the impact of the way you say it.

- Nido R Qubein

Profile of a Successful Entrepreneur

The Power of Effective Networking

I can tell you, without any doubt, that effective networking was and still is the number one factor in building my business because it was/is built on the foundation of trust.

When one of your underlying core values is integrity and never compromised, you cannot fail.

According to the *New World Dictionary,* networking is "the developing of contacts or exchanging of information with others in an informal network, as to further a career."

According to Coach Bud, networking is to "know your purpose, know your prospect profile, choose the event where they will be, and develop an in-person relationship founded on trust."

In this modern age, no technology will ever replace the power of face-to-face communication. Don't get me wrong about the value of technology. It has moved us way beyond what we would ever imagined and is just getting started.

However, we humans are social animals and need personal interaction to prosper. Some people are shy and feel uncomfortable in a group setting and walking up to someone they don't know to start a conversation.

That is understandable but can be overcome. It's all about using the process that I have found to work best. Let's go through that.

Effective Process:

1. Keep in mind that it's not about you; it's about them.

2. Ask and only tell when they ask you.

3. Develop your brief intro: I (we) help businesses (individuals) to...

4. Use one of the following approaches:

    a. Prospect does not have on name tag: "Hi; my name is Coach Bud. What's yours?" He says, "Joe." You say, "Joe, it's nice to meet you. What do you do?"

    b. Prospect has his/her name only on name tag: "Hi, Diane. I'm Coach Bud; it's nice to meet you. Diane, what is your business?"

    c. Prospect has name and name of his or her business on name tag: "Hi, Linda. I'm Coach Bud. I see you work with Steve's Bank. What are your responsibilities there?"

5. Continue asking follow-up questions to her responses.

6. At a point, she will ask you, Coach Bud, "Who do you coach?" The conversation is underway. Caution: If you have decided in your mind, that Joe, Diane, or Linda is not a prospect for you, don't overlook the fact that they may know someone who may be interested in doing business with you.

7. Follow Up: When both parties agree that you should have a one-on-one meeting to further explore opportunities to help each other, you take the responsibility to make that happen. Just saying, "Let's get together sometime" will not work. Sometime will never come. You schedule a later "coffee talk" right then or say you will contact them tomorrow—and do it! I prefer a coffee talk for the first meeting because you can get more done than lunch.

Strategic Alliance:

There is no better way to obtain a new client/customer than by getting a referral from someone you trust who opens the door to a prospect who in turn trusts the person who is referring you.

Trust is the key word in this transaction. Example of an ideal strategic alliance: You sell computer hardware and your trusted source sells computer software. You both call on the same prospect, but you are not competitive. The same client needs both of your products, so you agree with your trusted source to give him/her a referral to your clients and vice versa.

Well, a few months go by and you have given him/her five referrals and have gotten none in return. Very soon the relationship starts to dissolve. This is a common occurrence. The solution to this problem is simple.

Before you start the referral swapping, you sign a simple agreement that whoever gets a referral pays the referrer an agreed percent of the new client's billing for a year once the invoice is paid, deposited in the bank, and the payment clears.

Resource Center:

As soon as I started my business, I developed a list of trusted sources for both myself and my clients such as printers (people, not equipment), media sources, etc.

As this list grew, I had clients calling me and saying, "Coach Bud, I know you don't do this, but I know you can recommend someone that I can trust to do it right." Do you think that strengthens your relationship with your client? Duh!

Seek to know others. You'll be amazed at how it will help you understand yourself.

- Nido R Qubein

Go with the Pros

Work with professionals who risk and achieve things that others only dream about doing.

However, be aware of the negative: "I can do it all." One of the greatest strengths and weaknesses of an entrepreneur is the mindset that he or she can do everything. The positive "I can do it" attitude sometimes leads us to accept the "I can do it all" mindset, which can doom a business into the fate of over 400,000 businesses every year—failure.

In start-up mode, you may think you have to do it all because of limited financial resources. Even in those early days, you have to find a way to pay for those essential services that help you establish a foundation for success.

Most businesses budget expenditures for items such as rent, furniture, telephone, and other obvious necessities. However, money needs to be budgeted for accounting, legal, marketing, and other essential services that may not be so obvious.

One alternative method of funding your needs is the ancient tradition of barter. You can join one of the formal barter groups where you accumulate barter dollars by providing your products or services. In turn, you can spend those barter dollars on services and products you need. Or you can barter one-on-one; trading your offerings for the services you need without exchanging cash.

The caution here is to not pick your needed resource just because they will barter. However, if you find a resource person you feel sure can fulfill your needs and will barter, it can be a good way to preserve your cash flow.

Barter arrangements should always be treated as if it were a cash exchange.

If you do not possess the business skills and knowledge necessary to do your own accounting, legal work, marketing, selling, research, media selection and public relations, go with the pros.

If your brother-in-law is not a professional in any of those areas, don't let him convince you he can help you.

A growing trend of financial assistance is the concept of crowdfunding or crowdsourcing. Check this out by putting those terms in your search engine.

Before your heart beats too fast and your blood pressure elevates thinking you've got to win big in the Lottery to afford professional help, let's put this in perspective.

You do not have to hire high profile experts in the areas of your needs. There are entrepreneurs just like you in probably every area of expertise in services you need.

Spend time researching and find those professionals who, like you, understand the nuances of the entrepreneurial world. The best way to find these resources is from other entrepreneurs whose judgment you trust and who have a relationship with their recommended professionals.

Interview potential resource people to determine shared values and their competency. Look for more than their willingness to be a vendor. You want a partnership with someone who will show a genuine interest in you and believe in your product or service to help you grow your business.

If a potential resource is a member of the area chamber of commerce, chances are they are serious about their business.

Other sources of resources include trade associations, your bank, Better Business Bureau, and other professional organizations.

In your search for these resource relationships, keep in mind the true adage, "You get what you pay for."

Just as you are not likely to build a successful long-term business by being the lowest-priced guy in town neither are your resources.

Just as is the case with your customers, the value of a solid, long-term relationship is immeasurable. Invest the time to find these desired business relationships, nurture them, and you will grow your business.

In addition to your specific needs, you can add value to your client service by developing a bank of resources that you can recommend to your customers.

Be completely confident that anyone you recommend to your customer can meet their needs. For example, I have a long-standing relationship with a printing company that fulfills all my printed material needs and those of my clients.

Adding to the solid relationship is the fact they have a full-time graphic artist who is one of the best in the business. This relationship insures that working together we are going to produce an effective, quality product.

Incredibly, only about 5% of the people in America consistently commit to self-improvement by reading books and magazines, listening to audiotapes, watching videotapes, or attending seminars.

What an opportunity to differentiate yourself and company by committing to a lifetime of learning. There is a never-ending flow of resources to help you accelerate your journey of success.

In the fast-paced competitive marketplace we are all operating in, it is increasingly difficult for an entrepreneur to "go it alone." Building alliances with compatible (not competitive) companies who target the same market as you can open some of those locked doors not open to you and vice versa.

Most often the "I'll get you some leads and you get me some leads" scenario doesn't work. As time goes on the giving of leads gets out of balance and the person giving and not getting decides to stop giving.

To avoid this financial and emotional stress, establish *in writing* an agreement to pay a flat referral fee or a percent of billing to the referrer for a specified period of time. Under this arrangement, who gives whom the most referrals is not an issue. This is another benefit of your hard work in building your network of business contacts.

If you really want to see your business soar, let go of the "I can do it all" mindset and proactively seek resources that create win-win business arrangements.

May you achieve the success you *earn*!

Ordinary performers wait until they need help to seek advice. Extraordinary performers cultivate friendships with the experts before they need the expertise. Then, when they need help, it's readily available.

- Nido R Qubein

The 4 Ps of Successful Showcasing

One efficient and effective way to solidify (retain) your relationship with current customers and build (obtain) new relationships with prospective customers is to participate in trade shows and showcase exhibitions.

While a trade show is usually industry specific and most exhibitors are competitors, a showcase (often called an expo) is an event that hosts cross-industry participants.

Within certain industries, substantial transactions occur during a trade show.

Yet, a showcase, as its name implies, is designed to provide exhibitors an opportunity to showcase their products, services, and personnel in a positive light—and make four to five personal contacts per hour (according to national statistics).

Decision makers come to expos to look at and learn about the latest products and services. They don't usually come with pockets full of money or plastic to make purchases on the spot. Rather, they roam from booth to booth talking with exhibitors to assess whether certain products or services can help them be more efficient, effective, and profitable.

As an exhibitor, the purpose is to create a positive identity, meet face-to-face with current customers and qualified prospects, gather information to add to your database, and listen, not sell.

1. **Planning:**

    A. The first priority of the planning stage is to consider whether a particular showcase is the right match for your business. What is the expected attendance? What is the profile of an attendee? Does this profile match your target prospect?

    B. What is the scope of necessary resources (time, money, and people)? Make it a point to know all of these answers prior to making a commitment.

    C. Business expos are a business-to-business showcase. Thus, if your customers and target prospects are looking for business products, services, and possible new suppliers, this is probably a good match.

    D. By exhibiting, you not only "fill your pipeline" with qualified prospects, you can enhance your credibility and create a greater awareness of your company, its products, and services.

2. **Pre-Show:**

Okay, you've done your homework on the showcase and decided it is the right match. Now what?

It's time to create a checklist with a specific timeline of the activities you will need to conduct in the pre-show phase to ensure you fully leverage your involvement.

Statistics indicate that show success will be 50% greater when you conduct pre-show promotions.

Here are three key actions to consider:

- A. Invite your current customers and current prospects to attend the show and stop by your booth for a visit. Most expos provide tickets for exhibitors to distribute to clients and prospects.

- B. Utilize every communication method you already use to promote your participation and booth number. This includes your website (including show logo), social media, email signature, invoices, statements, advertising, voicemail greeting; on-hold messages, and all printed materials during the weeks leading up to the show.

- C. Basically, think outside the box and implement every creative way to promote your participation in the show.

3. **Presentation:**

    - A. Most expos allow you to set up your booth the day before the event opens. On show day, be at your booth at least a half hour before the doors open. Meet your neighbor exhibitors. The personnel staffing the booth must be thoroughly knowledgeable about the company and its products/services.

    - B. Booth visitors need to observe that your people are highly competent, reliable, responsive, and empathic to their needs.

    - C. There is a window of 3-5 seconds to capture the attention of the attendees as they pass by your booth.

D. The more compelling and inviting your booth is the better chance of attracting visitors.

E. Avoid aggressive methods of getting attendees into your booth. With a long day on a hard floor, you will want to work in two-to-three hour shifts two representatives at a time. Keeping a positive attitude is paramount to success. Conducting a prize(s) drawing at your booth is always good way to collect contact information to add to your database. Invite visitors to drop their business card in your receptacle for a chance to win.

F. This is also a good way to break the ice and engage the visitor in conversation. Caution: A big mistake people make is judging too quickly that the visitor is not a qualified prospect. They may not be a prospect, but someone they know might be.

G. Be sure your prize has value and appropriately represents your business.

H. Most shows prohibit "floor walkers" who have not purchased a booth yet attempt to sell their wares to exhibitors. Point out these offenders to show security, and they will be asked to leave the venue.

4. **Post-Show:**

Follow-up, follow-up, follow-up (get it?) is essential to your success. Send out a hand addressed "thank you for visiting our booth" letter immediately. Include the name(s) of prize winner(s). This enhances credibility. You may want to include a brochure. Review all of the contacts you personally made and decide the appropriate follow-up (i.e. phone call for appointment, regular mailings, etc.).

Have a meeting with all personnel who worked the booth as soon as possible to evaluate your results.

Track the business ultimately obtained from contacts made at the show. Be careful in making a snap judgment. Allow 30 days to pass. Attendees who weren't ready for your product or service immediately may contact you later.

In summary, if you follow the four Ps and maintain a positive attitude, you will probably realize the best return on any investment made this year.

CHAPTER FIVE
Advertising

What Is Advertising?

When you have your well-thought-out marketing plan finalized with your goals, it is time to consider which media you are going to use to reach your target market.

The answer is found in an effective process:

1. Be absolutely convinced that you have done all you can to objectively identify your target market. What is their profile?

2. *All* media have detailed research to determine their "target" market and will share that information with you. If you succeed with their media, they can sell more to other businesses.

3. If your target market matches that medium's target market and your message is also on target (3 Ms and 3 Cs of Communication), your chance of a successful outcome is greatly enhanced.

4. Be sure to budget sufficient funds to carry you through the early stages of your advertising campaign. It's a crowded field in any medium, and it takes a period of time for your market to see your message. Have patience. (Who, me?)

When you get a response to your advertising, follow up on that lead or you will have wasted your time and money.

When the infamous bank robber Willie Sutton was asked why he robbed banks, he simply replied, "That's where the money is."

Unlike marketing, advertising is money driven, not free.

Advertising Options

Print:

Local newspaper – Because newspaper is stationary, your message must follow the three Cs and three Ms. The reader will interpret your message by their understanding.

Specialty publications – These are usually subject focused, i.e., "Health & Happiness," etc. With less circulation than newspapers, the cost to advertise is much more reasonable. Be sure the publication is read by your target market.

Other – business cards, stationery, and specialty items such as pens, cups, etc. with your logo.

Audio: radio, podcasts

Consider format—country music, rock&roll, talk—when determining the appropriate outlet for you.

Audio/video

Television – Pick shows your prospects would watch.

Cablevision – smaller market, cost less than mainstream television

Social Media – Facebook, YouTube, Twitter, etc.

High-powered communicators focus words the way laser beams focus light.

- Nido R Qubein

CHAPTER SIX Sales

Universal Sales Purpose

Be a Solutionist

Selling is a Slam Dunk—with the Right Attitude

Fill the Pipeline

Universal Sales Purpose

"**To Build a positive relationship with your** clients/customers founded on trust, integrity, identification of needs, presentation of solutions and recommendation for action." —Coach Bud

Be a Solutionist

For some strange reason, *Webster's Dictionary* neither contains nor defines the term "solutionist."

However, in Coach Bud's entrepreneurs' glossary of terms, it is at the top of the list. In basic terms, a solutionist is one who provides solutions. Like a lot of concepts, it's a simple one to understand but often tough to implement. It often requires a complete change of mindset by everyone in the company—beginning at the top.

With any period of uncertain economic conditions, we all have to rethink ways to fulfill our purpose and keep our entrepreneurial spirit alive and well. Because an uncertain economy has a "filter down" effect on small and medium-sized businesses, we have to closely examine the strategy we implement.

Here is a strategy that, if you will truly embrace it, will better prepare you for the bad and good times.

When you become a solutionist, you add tremendous value to the relationship you have with your customer/client.

Buyers of products and services are looking for a solution for a need, want, or desire. They want someone to understand their situation and bring them solutions.

Another characteristic of these purchasers, particularly business-to-business, is they are extremely busy people (aren't we all). Typically, they don't have a lot of time to shop around for solutions.

This can be in your favor if you are a solutionist. The crowded, competitive marketplace requires us to discover a way to differentiate our company, our products/services, and ourselves. Otherwise, we find ourselves in a commodity market where the lowest price becomes the customer's highest priority.

Being the low-priced leader is not the reputation most of us are looking to create. Let's leave that to the WalMarts of the world.

Becoming a solutionist takes you out of the commodities market.

To further convince you to consider becoming a solutionist (are we there yet?), maybe the results of research conducted a few years ago will help.

A survey of 10,000 buyers across the United States gave a clear picture of what people want when they do business with you. In a nutshell, the results indicated buyers expect five things:

- **r**eliability (they can depend on you)

- **a**ssurance (you demonstrate trust and confidence),

- **t**angibles (neatness counts),

- **e**mpathy (understanding)

- **r**esponsiveness (be quick about it).

Notice something missing? You're right—price.

Now, let's put price in perspective. Meeting the five expectations doesn't mean you can charge a lot more than your competitors. However, it does mean that price is far less important *when you meet or exceed their expectations.*

Interestingly, when you put the first letter of each expectation together, it spells rater. Take a moment to rate your company in these five areas.

How well do you meet your customer's expectations?

"Okay, okay, enough," you say. "I am convinced that being a solutionist (24/7/365) will greatly enhance my success and position my company to ride out the tough times as well as the good times."

Great. You are now ready to adopt the "Pledge of the Solutionist."

Pledge of the Solutionist

1. I am 110% focused on the needs of my customers/prospects.

2. I will demonstrate by my actions that my customer is my top priority. I realize that when I help others succeed, I succeed.

3. I will ask my customer, "How are we doing for you?"

4. I will ask my customer, "What can we do to better serve your needs?"

Congratulations, now that you have adopted the pledge, it's time to establish it as the fundamental foundation of your company's culture.

For this to work, every person in your company must embrace the pledge.

More importantly, every person must demonstrate they can live by the pledge.

Master Solutionist: Are you ready for this? If you want to be a master solutionist, you build a vast network of qualified, trusted resources and become a resource center for your customers.

For example, if your expertise is in software development and your client expresses the need for additional hardware, you can recommend a resource to fulfill that need.

Remember: When you recommend a resource, your relationship with your customer is on the line. Your recommendation better be someone you have complete trust and confidence in to fulfill the customer's needs.

When you earn the trust of your clients enough so that they ask you for resources outside your immediate expertise, it doesn't get much better than that.

In the example cited above, you may want to extend that resource into an alliance. An alliance in this context means formalizing an agreement with a preferred hardware provider. The written agreement can simply be an agreement to open the door to each other's clients who have a need for the other's expertise. This arrangement should not be simply, "You give me some leads and I'll give you some." This doesn't work.

Very quickly who *gives* and who *gets* can become out of balance. If this occurs, relationships are strained. When you have a reciprocal financial arrangement with a specified percentage (typically 10-20%) of billing going to the person who opens the door to the client, the issue of who gives the most leads is not a factor.

When you become a solutionist, you differentiate yourself from the seemingly infinite number of competitors.

You build a strong, lasting relationship with your customers. And you have fun doing it.

Profile of a Successful Entrepreneur

The surest route today is to find out what others want and look for ways to provide it.

- Nido R Qubein

Bud (Coach Bud) Coggins

Selling is a Slam Dunk — with the Right Attitude!

How many of you can't wait to get up in the morning and rush out to sell your product/service?

That's usually the first question I ask in my sales seminar designed for entrepreneurs and non-sales people. Maybe one or two hands will raise.

The fact is most people have a negative perception of selling. They associate selling with being manipulative and using aggressive tactics. A career in sales is something you hope your brother-in-law, who hasn't had a steady job in five years, wouldn't even consider doing.

Unfortunately, this perception is enhanced by movie and television portrayals of either a buffoon such as Herb Tarlek of *WKRP in Cincinnati*, a slick-talking conman like Professor Harold Hill in *The Music Man* or Willie Loman in *Death of a Salesman*.

Let me be quick to add that these characters do exist in the real world. They most often prey on the innocent and the elderly. But the truth is these lowlifes are distinctly in the minority.

On the other hand, hundreds of thousands of professionally-trained salespeople hit the streets every day in our country to offer products and services that fuel our economic engines. Just once I would like to see a news headline that reads, "Sally Salesperson Helps Clients Become More Efficient and Productive."

Most people who start their own businesses have little to no training or experience in sales. They usually start a business for one of three reasons:

1. They (entrepreneurs) sincerely have a passion for independence and making a difference in the lives of others by providing products or services that enhance quality of life or will help a business be more profitable.

2. They (business owners) are tired of working for someone else and think they can do better with their own business.

3. They (laid off) decide to make a go on their own rather than pursue employment.

Unfortunately, statistics indicate that those who strike out on their own for reasons two and three listed above are more likely to be among the 400,000 businesses that fail each year.

If you own a business or are thinking of starting one, a *must read* is *The E-Myth Revisited* by Michael E. Gerber. (No, I don't get any commission on book sales.)

The catch-22 for most start-up business owners is that their lack of experience in selling and limited financial resources to hire professional salespeople can result in failure of a new business.

Since limited financial resources tends to inhibit sales production, the most prudent course is to acquire the necessary knowledge and skills to help customers buy your product or service.

The good news is that you can develop the attitude and acquire the skills to be successful with a dedication to self-development.

How do you begin? You start by developing a positive mindset about selling. Take the word selling out of your vocabulary and focus on matching your customer's needs with solutions provided by your product or service. Consider yourself a solutionist instead of a salesperson.

There is nothing manipulative about providing a product or service that meets the challenges of your customers and prospects.

There is still a misperception that you have to be a card-carrying extrovert to be successful in selling. That may have been true in Willie Loman's day but not today.

Created by our era of information overload, the buying public is too smart and sophisticated to fall for a manipulative con game.

Once you embrace a positive attitude and consider yourself a solutionist, you must add a large dose of trustworthiness. Personal growth author Stephen Covey defines this as earning the trust and confidence of your customer and being competent in your chosen work.

With those principles, you also need a few skills to help raise your success level. I recommend you pick up a copy of *SPIN Selling* by Neil Rackham (still no commission).

After 12 years of research and observing 35,000 sales calls, Rackham and his associate researchers determined what really works in the real world selling process.

The biggest challenge in today's crowded marketplace is identifying the decision maker and getting an appointment with that person. That is why building a vast network of business contacts and creating a referral system is so essential to your success.

When someone with whom you have established trustworthiness can open a prospect's door for you, it can't get any better than that.

Your toughest competition is not someone who offers a similar product or service as yours. Your toughest competition is getting time with the decision maker and the expendable dollars the customer has available.

Reading and applying the process outlined in *SPIN Selling* will give you a direction to meet these challenges.

In summary, if you maintain a positive attitude, establish trustworthiness, become an avowed solutionist, and follow the proven process outlined in *SPIN Selling*, you will be one of the people who raises his or her hand when someone asks, "Who can't wait to get up in the morning and go out and offer your product/service?"

Success, significance, and achievement don't depend on what we do; they depend on who we are.

- Nido R Qubein

Fill the Pipeline…24/7/365

The selling profession has a long-standing mantra: "Fill the pipeline."

This reflects the reality of the length and nuances of the sales cycle.

The length of the sales cycle is always longer than the salesperson or entrepreneur expects or wants it to be. The reasons for this include delayed buying decisions, not being able to have discussions with the actual decision maker, an *unsold* buyer, or a myriad of other issues.

Who hasn't been sure that a sale would go through only to find out that the deal is not happening at all? A deal is only done when the product/service has been transferred to the customer, invoiced, and the payment is securely in your bank account.

Hence, ensuring that a large number of qualified prospects are in your pipeline during all the various stages of the sales cycle is critical.

Whether you want to think of it as a numbers game or not, it is. Business-to-business statistics indicate that one in 16 qualified prospects will result in obtaining a customer. In a slowed economy, this ratio is probably wider.

Filling your pipeline with qualified prospects is essential to your success.

Another nuance of the selling process is the fact that, increasingly, decision makers are far less likely to respond to your voicemail message or grant an appointment to someone with whom they are unfamiliar.

Even those who do know you may not respond to your voicemail message.

Always attempt to reach the decision maker *live* at least twice before leaving a message. When you must leave a message, be sure it is compelling (not conniving) enough to get a returned call. Take care not to make exaggerated claims in your message.

So what is a salesperson or entrepreneur to do? The single most important activity is constantly building your network of business contacts. While this is most often a slower process than you would like, it is the most effective.

In the past it was who you knew that made the difference. In today's business world, it's also who knows you.

Your communication strategy needs to combine traditional marketing tactics with innovative ideas utilizing appropriate technology to create a positive identity for you, your product/service, and your company. This strategy must target a list of qualified prospects in your pipeline.

Okay, how do you fill your pipeline? First, you dispel the notion that everyone in your pipeline must be a prospect. They may not be; however, who they know may be valuable to you.

A common mistake is going to a networking event, meeting someone and deciding instantly that they are obviously not a prospect and, therefore, moving on.

You may have just missed a good referral source. It's called "tap rooting."

Second, recognize the most effective marketing is to have someone else recommend you. Your current customers often are willing to help you obtain new customers once you demonstrate your competency and earn their trust—but only if you ask.

Make it a point to ask your current customers, "How are we doing for you?" or "What can we do to better serve your needs?"

Once you have confirmed that they are more than satisfied with your service or product, you are in a position to ask them for a referral. Always ask them if it's okay to use their name as a referral source.

Build up a bank of clients who are willing to act as references you can share with your new prospects.

As if there weren't already enough reasons to take care of and retain your current clients, they are your best source of obtaining new clients—when they are a raving fan of yours.

Third, maintain of list of 25 people who can positively influence your success. This list should contain actual prospects as well as others who can, through their contacts, open doors for you.

Realize that in the crowded, competitive marketplace of today, it is virtually impossible for entrepreneurs to go it alone. Compatible alliances are a must for survival. Even the "big boys" are merging or partnering for their survival.

In the best alliances, each party maintains their unique identity and can be introduced as a potential partner or subcontractor to the customer. To avoid a strained or failed alliance, work out a mutually agreeable financial arrangement with your strategic partner.

Providing the partner with a fixed finder's fee or percent of billing will avoid the almost always doomed idea of "you get me some leads and I will get you some."

Finally, each week set quantifiable goals to contact a certain number of current customers, dormant customers, prospects, and possible alliances.

Typically, contact does not refer to mass mailings. Whatever method of contact you plan to use, be sure you have allowed for timely follow-up. For example, if you write a one-page letter briefly describing why you think you can fill a prospect's needs and you commit to a follow-up phone call within a week, be sure you make that call.

As they say in the real estate business, the three most important factors are location, location, location. In marketing and selling, it's follow-up, follow-up, follow-up.

Your marketing and selling strategy is only effective when you include dedication to follow-up.

Resolve today to proactively build a vast network of business contacts. This single activity will significantly raise you to a higher level of success.

CHAPTER SEVEN
Customer Service

The Customer Is Boss or You Are Fired.

Customer service is exceeding customer expectations and providing those unexpected, little touches that make a big difference.

As in any lasting relationship, you must earn the trust of your customers. It is incumbent upon you to instill confidence in them that you and your company possess the competency to provide successful solutions.

In today's crowded, competitive marketplace, you have to find ways to prevent customers and prospects from perceiving your products/services as commodities.

In a commodity market, price becomes the determining factor for making their purchase. I don't know any entrepreneurs whose dream it is to be known as the lowest price guy in town.

It is amazing how simple the concept of delivering superior customer service is and how apparently difficult it is to deliver. It doesn't have to be that way. When you develop and maintain a mindset that the customer is your number one priority, you develop a customer service culture that becomes a way of life. This ultimately determines the company's success.

It is interesting how the slowed economy and the tragic events of 9/11 have precipitated some renewal of customer service. We are certainly not in a customer service renaissance, but any awareness of the value of a customer is a good thing.

History has shown us that, unfortunately, as business starts improving and more customers are available, the value of the customer seems to diminish.

As Benjamin Disraeli said over 150 years ago, "The secret of success is consistency of purpose."

When we establish a consistent, superior customer service culture, we are able to retain customers and give them an incentive to help us obtain more.

To further reinforce the value of customer service, consider the following research findings from a survey designed to find out why customers quit doing business with a company.

The survey revealed that...

- 1% die
- 3% move away
- 5% develop other friendships
- 9% leave for competitive reasons
- 14% are dissatisfied with product, and
- 68% quit because they perceived an attitude of indifference by the owner, manager, or an employee.

Ouch! Sixty-eight percent stop doing business because they feel the company does not value them as a customer? Inexcusable? Yes! Avoidable? Yes!

The survey goes on to point out that the typical company hears from only 4% of its dissatisfied customers. The other 96% just go quietly away, and 91% of those customers will never come back.

This should not be surprising when you realize that human nature is to avoid adversarial situations and, more importantly, customers do have other choices of companies that provide the same products and services.

There is one absolute fact of customer service. The person at the top of the company is the one who sets the foundation for delivering superior customer service. That person must understand, believe, and live by these principles:

1. Demonstrate by actions that customer's needs are above all else.
2. Empower employees to solve customer dissatisfaction on the spot.
3. Demonstrate by actions that employees are your best customers.
4. Remember that customers always have a choice (applies to all but the IRS).
5. Insure the lines of communication with customers (internal and external) are always open.
6. Invest in customer service skills training for everyone in the company.
7. Focus on retaining your customers, and they will help you obtain others.
8. Understand that the customer may not always be right, but they are the boss.

There are many good resources for learning more about the value of customers and ways to deliver superior customer service.

The window of opportunity is wide open to differentiate you and your company from the crowded, competitive marketplace by delivering superior customer service.

Demonstrate to your customers that you value them by treating them as royalty, and you will grow and prosper.

In the marketplace of life, the seller may set the price, but it is always the buyer who determines the value.

- Nido R Qubein

ASSESSMENT

Entrepreneur Compatibility Self-Assessment

This Compatibility Assessment is designed to help you decide if you match the characteristics of a successful entrepreneur. The value of this process is based on the honest objectivity of your responses. Please circle your response (1 lowest, 10 highest). Rate where you are now on each characteristic. For current entrepreneurs, this is a checklist.

If my journey is to be successful I must have…

1. A written **PURPOSE STATEMENT** of my business

    1 2 3 4 5 6 7 8 9 10

2. An **UNCOMPROMISING PASSION** for my purpose

    1 2 3 4 5 6 7 8 9 10

3. Completed **DUE DILIGENCE** in determining my market potential

   1 2 3 4 5 6 7 8 9 10

4. A **WRITTEN BUSINESS PLAN** outlining specific goals

   1 2 3 4 5 6 7 8 9 10

5. **SUFFICIENT FUNDING** and **CASH FLOW PROJECTIONS**

   1 2 3 4 5 6 7 8 9 10

6. A **CLEAR VISION** of the future

   1 2 3 4 5 6 7 8 9 10

7. A strong belief in my **CORE VALUES**

   1 2 3 4 5 6 7 8 9 10

8. **EFFECTIVE COMMUNICATIONS**

   1 2 3 4 5 6 7 8 9 10

9. A **VAST NETWORK** of personal and business contacts

   1 2 3 4 5 6 7 8 9 10

10. A development of **STRATEGIC ALLIANCES**

    1 2 3 4 5 6 7 8 9 10

11. **EARNED** the **TRUST** of **OTHERS**

    1 2 3 4 5 6 7 8 9 10

12. Experience in **MARKETING**

    1 2 3 4 5 6 7 8 9 10

13. Experience in **SALES**

    1 2 3 4 5 6 7 8 9 10

14. A **CUSTOMER-FOCUSED** attitude

    1 2 3 4 5 6 7 8 9 10

15. A **TARGETED ADVERTISING/MARKETING** plan

    1 2 3 4 5 6 7 8 9 10

16. Resources to **UTILIZE CURRENT TECHNOLOGIES**

    1 2 3 4 5 6 7 8 9 10

17. Commitment to **GIVE BACK** to community

    1 2 3 4 5 6 7 8 9 10

18. A written plan for **PHYSICAL** and **MENTAL FITNESS**

   1 2 3 4 5 6 7 8 9 10

19. A plan for **SELF DEVELOPMENT**

   1 2 3 4 5 6 7 8 9 10

20. A specific **EXIT STRATEGY**

   1 2 3 4 5 6 7 8 9 10

Note:

This Entrepreneur Compatibility Self-Assessment is the property of CoachBudsEntrepreneursU and is intended for the exclusive use of the reader. It may not be reproduced without written permission from CoachBudsEntrepreneursU.

Special Offer:

After you have read this book and completed your Self-Assessment, if have questions there is an option for you.

Coach Bud offers a one-on-one confidential telephone consulting opportunity.

An hourly rate is usually $120.00, but your rate will be $80. Should you choose to take advantage of this special offer, go to www.coachbudsbooks.com and sign up.

www.ingramcontent.com/pod-product-compliance
Lightning Source LLC
Chambersburg PA
CBHW052200110526
44591CB00012B/2015